I WANT TO BE . . . Book Series
Creator/Producer: Stephanie Maze of Maze Productions, Inc.
Writer and Educational Consultant: Catherine O'Neill Grace
Designer: Alexandra Littlehales

Photographers for I WANT TO BE A CHEF:
Annie Griffiths Belt, Nicole Bengevino, Ira Block, Sam Kittner,
John A. Gastaldo, Karen Kasmauski, Richard T. Nowitz, Robert Clark,
Susan C. Bourgoin, Renee Comet, Steve Mellon, James A. Sugar.

Other books available in this series:
I WANT TO BE AN ASTRONAUT
I WANT TO BE A DANCER
I WANT TO BE AN ENGINEER
I WANT TO BE A FIREFIGHTER
I WANT TO BE A VETERINARIAN

Requests for permission to make copies
of any part of the work should be mailed to:
Permissions Department, Harcourt Brace & Company,
6277 Sea Harbor Drive, Orlando, Florida 32887-6777.

Photography and recipe credits appear on page 48.

Library of Congress Cataloging-in-Publication Data
Maze, Stephanie.
I want to be a chef/creator/producer Stephanie Maze; writer and educational
consultant Catherine O'Neill Grace—1st ed.
p. cm.—(I want to be—book series)
"A Maze Productions book."
Summary: Describes some of the careers in the culinary arts, including master chef,
executive chef, pastry chef, prep chef, and more, and discusses the training,
vocabulary, competitions, and possibilities in this field.
ISBN 0-15-201864-6   ISBN 0-15-201936-7 pb
1. Cooks—Juvenile literature.
2. Cookery—Vocational guidance—Juvenile literature.
[1. Cookery—Vocational guidance. 2. Cooks. 3. Occupations.
4. Vocational guidance] I. Grace, Catherine O'Neill, 1950– .
II. Title. III. Series.
TX652.5.M3551 1999
641.5'023—dc21 98-3906

First edition
A C E F D B
A C E F D B (pb)

Film processing by A & 1 Color, Los Angeles
Pre-press through PrintNet, San Francisco
Printed and bound by Tien Wah Press, Singapore

I Want to Be...

A CHEF

A Maze Productions Book

HARCOURT BRACE & COMPANY

SAN DIEGO   NEW YORK   LONDON

ACKNOWLEDGMENTS

We wish to thank the following people, companies, and institutions for their very valuable contributions to this book: Chef Mark Miller of Coyote Cafe, Santa Fe, New Mexico; Chef David Keener of Ridgewell's Caterers, Washington, D.C.; the Culinary Institute of America; the American Culinary Federation; and Johnson & Wales University.

Many thanks, also, to the following restaurants of the greater Washington, D.C., area: La Chaumiere, Marrakesh, the Grill from Ipanema, Germaine's, Mykonos, Old Europe, Bombay Palace, Nam-Viet Pho-79, Zed's, Andalucia, Cactus Cantina, I Matti, Sushi-Ko, and Firehook Bakery.

And finally, our heartfelt gratitude to all the professionals in this book for allowing us to interrupt their busy schedules and for agreeing to be the wonderful role models children can look up to for many years to come.

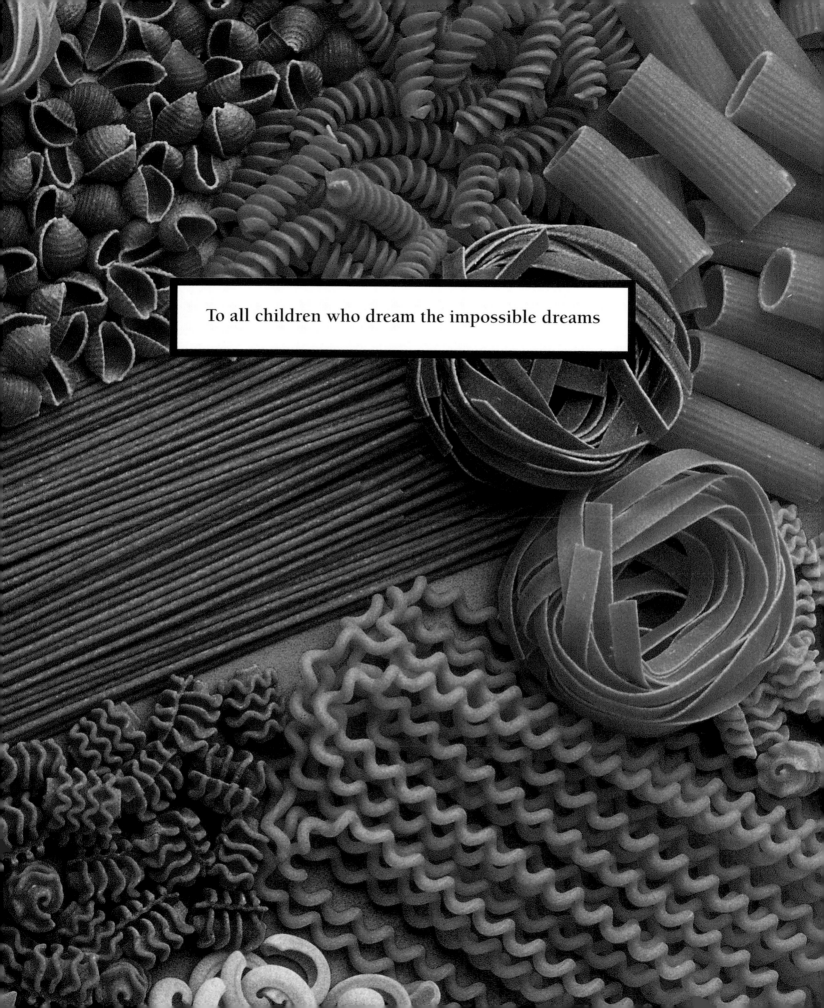

To all children who dream the impossible dreams

Where to Start

Do you love to eat? Are you adventurous about eating foods from other countries? Do you enjoy trying out new recipes on your family and friends? Are you comfortable in the kitchen? You may have what it takes to become a professional chef.

Becoming a chef can take years of training. Some people learn as apprentices in famous restaurants. Others attend culinary colleges. However a chef trains, he or she soon discovers that professional cooking is hard work that requires long hours and lots of physical stamina. It's also creative, exciting, and tons of fun. After all, you get to eat your work! Plus, cooking is a profession that's growing fast. Experts at the United States Bureau of Labor Statistics say that by the year 2005, the demand for trained chefs will exceed the supply—so it should be easy to find good jobs.

Where could you work as a chef? You might find a position in a hotel kitchen, like the one at the Hyatt Regency on Capitol Hill in Washington, D.C., where banquet chef Edward Deng (center) and his colleagues prepare a colorful vegetable dish for a luncheon. Cook David Arias (left) and chef saucier Antonio Saene (right) assist him, as cook Tyrone White (background) stands by, ready to lend a hand. Everyone's busy. The hungry banquet guests are beginning to arrive in the dining room!

Executive chef

Master chef

Chef-Owner

Hands-on. *Master chef Ronald DeSantis (above) teaches at St. Andrew's Café, a student-staffed restaurant at the Culinary Institute of America in Hyde Park, New York. Master chefs hold highly specialized degrees in the culinary arts. At left, chef Douglas Rodriguez adds a special touch to the Cuban American specialties he serves at his New York City restaurant, Patria.*

Types of Chefs

In French, the word *chef* means chief or boss. For us, a chef is the chief cook—the boss—in the kitchen where he or she is employed. But professional food preparation involves many people who do different things. The prep cook slices piles of vegetables, cleans mounds of salad greens, and chops dozens of heads of garlic. The pastry assistant readies ingredients for baked goods and helps arrange fancy desserts just before they're served. The garde-manger sets out cold foods, while cooks on the "hot line" prepare meat and fish dishes that are served hot. The pastry chef bakes bread, makes custards, sorbets, and ice cream, and also creates cakes and other baked treats.

Luckily there's also a dishwasher who keeps the pots, pans, utensils, and dishes from piling up too high. The sous-chef helps the chef run the kitchen and does lots of cooking. And at the head of the team, there's the chef, who plans menus, cooks special items, and makes sure that everyone works together.

In a large operation, such as New York City's Four Seasons Hotel, an executive chef is in charge of the entire kitchen operation—from supervising the staff to deciding what will be on the daily menus. Everything must work smoothly. Four Seasons' executive chef Susan Weaver—shown in large photo at left, with cook Persio Almonte, checks a simmering cauldron of vegetable stock for soup. She is one of the few women in the United States to hold the title of executive chef.

Garde-manger

Hotel restaurant chef

Pastry chef

On the line. *At the Capitol Hyatt Regency in Washington, D.C., garde-manger Edwina Johnson prepares salads for lunch (top); chef James Ware sets up the salad bar at the hotel restaurant (above center); and (above) pastry chef Yong Han (right) and pastry assistant Christopher Pulling (left) decorate desserts for a banquet.*

A Morning with a Pastry Chef

It's still dark in Washington, D.C., as world-famous pastry chef Dieter Schorner arrives at his restaurant, Patisserie Café Didier.

"Pastry chefs usually start early—five A.M. or even earlier," Chef Dieter explains. "The first thing you make is breakfast. After all, that's what people eat first!"

Chef Dieter heats up his ovens. He takes the croissant dough he made the day before out of the refrigerator and sets it aside to rise. Then he starts putting together the ingredients for Danish pastries, muffins, scones, and brioche.

"Everything needs to be ready for hungry customers at eight o'clock," he says. What's his favorite breakfast pastry? "I love Danishes because I do them as I learned in Scandinavia. They are light and flaky."

Chef Dieter has been rising early to create wonderful pastries for many years. "My family was very poor during World War II. A school friend of mine knew a baker. 'I will give you bread, but you must come very early in the morning,' the baker offered. So ever since I was ten years old, I have worked in a bakery."

After an apprenticeship in Germany, Chef Dieter went to one of the best pastry schools in Switzerland. Later he worked as a pastry chef on luxury cruise ships, for the Swedish royal family, and at famous hotels in England. Today he is the owner of Café Didier and teaches pastry making at the French Culinary Institute in New York City.

As the morning light streams into the kitchen, Chef Dieter takes hot pastries out of the oven. Their aroma fills the small café. Soon his customers will begin to stop in on their way to work, hungry for coffee and fresh croissants.

But Chef Dieter's work isn't finished for the day. As his customers arrive to eat breakfast, he's already busy again, baking bread, pastries, and cake to serve with lunch.

Busy morning. *Long before most people are awake, pastry chef Dieter Schorner and his assistant, Jaime Molina, are hard at work. They mix batter (top left) for a batch of muffins that the breakfast crowd will devour in a couple of hours. Chef Dieter measures dough (bottom left) that will be set aside to rise and later be made into flaky croissants. He then uses a pastry bag to form ladyfinger cookies (above right). His assistant sifts confectioners' sugar to decorate the top of a fruit pastry (above center). Chef Dieter arranges cinnamon raisin danishes and apple turnovers on paper doilies (right) for display in the bakery case.*

Education and Training

Lunchtime is busy when you cook for a crowd. Above, chef-instructor Clay Doubleday watches sous-chef (and high school student) Nick Statanias check orders at Chantilly Professional Technical Center, a high school in Chantilly, Virginia, where teenagers learn the food service business, including preparing vegetables and other ingredients, cooking, and waiting on tables. Many students from this program go on to cooking school—often with scholarships.

Not too long ago, cooking instruction at school was confined to home economics classes for girls. But now schools around the country offer hands-on classes to teach boys and girls about food and cooking. For example, at Patrick Henry Elementary School in Arlington, Virginia, nutrition is part of the science curriculum. At Franklin Middle School in Chantilly, Virginia, boys and girls take cooking classes together.

Community colleges also run programs for aspiring chefs. Northern Virginia Community College and the Nation's Capital Chef's Association together offer an apprentice program that mixes classwork with on-the-job training.

Good for you. *At Patrick Henry Elementary School (below), science teacher Celez Nitkowski shows students (from left) Amy Walton, Jaimie Danielson, Monica Kelly, and Mudib Rawoot how to choose heart-healthy foods by reading nutrition labels.*

Learning by doing. *At Northern Virginia Community College (above), instructor Benita Wong shows students Sheronda Gayle and John Rogers how to use aspic. Aspic—a jelly made from meat or fish stock, or fruit or vegetable juice—is used to create fancy molded salads and other dishes. At Franklin Middle School (right), students simulate a professional kitchen by working as a team.*

13

The Culinary Institute of America

When aspiring chefs hear the acronym *CIA*, they think of famous chefs, not famous spies! That's because in the cooking world there's only one CIA: the prestigious Culinary Institute of America, in Hyde Park, New York. Founded in 1946, the CIA has graduated more than thirty thousand students, all of whom received the medal shown above left—a prized symbol of their accomplishment.

The CIA offers continuing education classes for professional and amateur cooks. The school also awards associate's and bachelor's degrees. Admission to the degree programs is competitive, just as it is at liberal arts or other professional colleges. Applicants must get a recommendation from someone who knows how they work with food. So if you want to go to the CIA, you have to get at least three months of food service experience first. Once you're enrolled, you'll get lots of hands-on training. Above, students put together platters of hors d'oeuvres under the watchful eye of an assistant professor nearby.

CIA students take classes in a range of

subjects, including breakfast cookery (they have to get up at three A.M. for that class!), food science, and the secrets of cuisines from many cultures. At top right, students knead dough in a bread-making class taught by associate professor Richard Coppedge.

At right center, John Nunziata perfects his serving technique. CIA students also work in all four of the college's public restaurants. Would you like to sample their food? Then check out the CIA's American Bounty Restaurant or the Caterina de Medici Dining Room, both in Hyde Park, New York. Students also train at other restaurants. Mark Williams (bottom right) cooks at The Beekman 1776 Tavern in Rhinebeck, New York.

CIA students have their pick of jobs after graduation. According to the *Wall Street Journal*, each of the school's twelve hundred annual graduates receives an average of three job offers.

Sweet exam. *Jason Derr and Jennifer Berdych take a cake-decorating test (above). Later, they carry their creations to the dorm to share with classmates.*

Other Programs

Are you a chocolate-chip cookie chef? Does your pizza have pizzazz? If you love cooking, you might want to participate in after-school or weekend cooking programs.

Trying out your cooking in a local Boy or Girl Scout program is a good way to sharpen your skills. Many girls and boys take pride in sewing cooking badges on their Scout merit badge sashes. Or you can attend summer cooking camps. You can also learn to cook in a time-honored way: in your kitchen at home.

The kids sampling cake batter in the photo at top right are attending a summer cooking camp for eight- to thirteen-year-olds at L'Académie de Cuisine in Bethesda, Maryland. The cooking school—which also offers programs for adults, as well as classes that parents and kids take together—runs fun courses for kids year-round. For Halloween, there's a spooky cookie class. At Christmastime, kids can take a gingerbread-house workshop. In basic technique classes at the academy, kids learn to cook meals they can re-create at home. They're menus that kids enjoy. How would you like to concoct salsa to serve with chips, make beef kebabs with peppers and onions, and bake an apple crisp for your family—and then surprise them when you say you made the meal from scratch?

Pies, cakes, and cookies are the specialties of the LaBreque household in Purcellville, Virginia. At right center, Amanda LaBreque carefully removes a cake from the oven. Her mom, Violet,

Stirring session. *Chef Harvey Boyd (above) demonstrates mixing at the Kids' Café, an after-school program at the Southwest Boys and Girls Club in Orlando, Florida. Area chefs volunteer their time to teach kids about cooking.*

watches in the background. Amanda, twelve, and her sister, Elizabeth, eight, have won lots of blue ribbons for their baking with their mom's help. (Check out one of their prizewinning entries on page 30.) When the girls were younger, Mrs. LaBreque taught them how to bake and entered contests with them. Now she thinks both daughters have become accomplished enough at baking to enter county fairs on their own.

Would you like to try cooking at home? There are lots of cookbooks written with kids in mind. Check some out from your local library or buy one at a bookstore and get started. But remember, if you decide to try any of the recipes, always ask for permission first. And don't forget to ask a grown-up to help you whenever your recipe calls for using a hot stove or a sharp knife.

In the photo at right, Christopher Calder, eleven, sharpens a carving knife as chef Mark Davis supervises. Christopher is taking part in a weekend cooking class at the California Culinary Academy in San Francisco, California. In the hands-on program, Chef Davis teaches kids how to make pizza dough—and toss it in the air like professional pizzeria chefs. Students concoct homemade pizza sauce, too. The students master basic techniques, such as slicing and sautéing, and learn to create beautiful desserts. They also learn about presentation, the art of making food look attractive. At the end of the program, they cook and serve a banquet to an appreciative crowd: their parents.

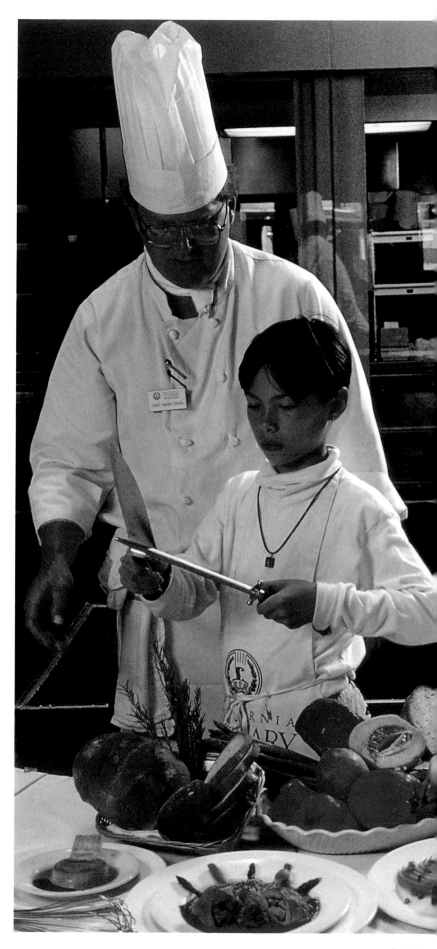

The History of the Culinary Arts

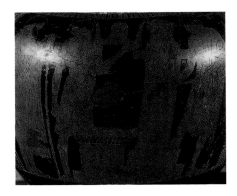

What's one thing you have in common with cave people? You need food to survive, just as they did. Since prehistoric people discovered fire, cooks have been important members of society. Archaeologists have found charred animal bones and roasted seeds and grains at some of the oldest campfire sites.

As civilizations have developed and changed, so has cooking. (Thank goodness! You probably wouldn't find the woolly mammoth meat that cave people dined on very appetizing.) And as different cultures have interacted through trade or immigration, food habits have changed, too. Take corn, for example. A staple food for Native Americans, corn was unknown in Europe, Asia, and Africa until after Christopher Columbus brought it to Spain from the New World in 1492. European explorers also brought back to their parts of the globe potatoes, chocolate, and tomatoes from the Americas. These new foods often became popular! Can you imagine Irish food without potatoes? Or Swiss desserts without chocolate? Or Italian food without tomatoes? All of these countries have the Americas to thank for their most-loved dishes. In fact, before the fifteenth century, Italians topped pasta with vegetables, cheese, and cream—not "red sauce."

On an ancient Greek vase, men sacrifice food to Hermes, messenger of the gods (top left). Above, an Egyptian mural (1314–1197 B.C.) shows Queen Nefertari carrying food to the gods. Below, a detail of a twentieth-century mural by Mexican artist Diego Rivera depicts Aztecs selling corn in the marketplace.

Many of our favorite food-plants were first cultivated in Asia, Africa, and Europe. Wheat, oats, barley, and rice were first raised and eaten in Asia. Apples, grapes, pears, and peaches originated in Europe. (Put together Asian wheat and European apples, and what do you get? American apple pie!)

The men and women who figured out how to turn these foodstuffs into tasty things to eat have played a significant role in society for thousands of years. Prepared food was so important to the Egyptians that it was put into a deceased person's grave to provide sustenance in the afterlife.

Cooks started writing down their recipes long ago. One of the earliest cookbooks was written in Latin in the fourth century. During the Middle Ages, cooks in Europe began to form organizations called guilds to share information and support one another. This is how a fourteenth-century guild manual describes a master chef: "He is a cook. He takes fowl from the air; fish from the waters; fruits, vegetables, and grain from the land; and animals that walk

In the 1400s, a cook stirs a pot over an open fire (top left). A griddle with spits made things easier in the 1500s (top center). Italian artist and inventor Leonardo da Vinci had a better idea: an automatic steam-driven spit (top right).

Kitchen life. *Above, a 1566 Flemish painting called "Farmer's Feast" shows a crowded peasant kitchen. At right, a portrait painted in 1574 depicts a woman preparing chicken to be roasted.*

Tools of the trade. *A humorous eighteenth-century cartoon shows a chef dressed in his equipment (above left). In an 1878 caricature, a French chef wears the traditional toque, white jacket, and striped pants of his profession (above right). Below, a home cook uses a coal stove while her dog enjoys the heat. The stove was invented in the United States in 1800 and quickly replaced open-hearth cooking.*

the earth, and through his skills and art transforms the raw product to edible food." Sounds a lot like what chefs do today, doesn't it?

In the sixteenth century, when Princess Catherine de Médicis of Florence, Italy, moved to France to marry the future king, she took her own chefs with her—as well as her own forks, since the French used their fingers along with knives at that time. The Florentines influenced French cooking, which soon became the most famous in the world. The first formal restaurants opened in France in the 1700s.

A well-known French chef, Auguste Escoffier (opposite page, top right), who lived from 1846 to 1935, improved restaurant efficiency by inventing the brigade system.

In the 1800s, French cuisine became very influential. Even in the United States, President Thomas Jefferson had a French chef. (In fact, most White House chefs were French or cooked in the French style until President Bill Clinton moved into the White House in 1994 and hired American chefs.)

In the United States, television has helped turn some chefs into well-known personalities. Julia Child and James Beard (pictured together at far right, center), were two of the first celebrity chefs. Both have published best-selling cookbooks and appeared on popular TV shows. Today millions of Americans watch cooking shows—and try out new recipes—every week.

In the late twentieth century, the trademark of American cooking has been the use of fresh, locally grown ingredients—a practice begun in

the 1970s by Alice Waters, chef-owner of Chez Panisse in Berkeley, California. American cooking also has borrowed ingredients from many cultures, including Chinese and Italian, Japanese and Scandinavian, Greek and Irish, Jamaican and Indian, African and Vietnamese. Some of the best American cooking today is influenced by these rich culinary traditions from abroad.

Alexis Soyer (1810–1858) (above left) ran a food kitchen that fed more than a million people during the Irish potato famine. Fannie Merritt Farmer (1857–1915) (above center) published the Boston Cooking School Cook Book, the first cookbook to specify amounts for measured ingredients.

Smiling staff. *At Chez Panisse, Alice Waters is surrounded by her staff of cooks who specialize in creating menus according to a simple principle. Use foods that are "fresh, local, and seasonal," Waters says—like the fish and produce on the kitchen table at right. Waters, who is credited with creating "California cuisine," is the author of several books, including* The Chez Panisse Menu Cookbook *and* Fanny at Chez Panisse, *a storybook and cookbook for children.*

Cooking and Technology

Modern chefs are quick to use new technologies. David Keener (small photo, far left below), the executive chef for Ridgewell's, a catering business in Bethesda, Maryland, brought new menus—and new technology—to the traditional company. After perfecting his recipe for caramelized banana brioche pudding, Keener composes the step-by-step instructions on his laptop computer.

Lespinasse, a French restaurant in Washington, D.C. (large photo), has a state-of-the-art kitchen with an induction cooktop that doesn't feel hot—even when it's turned up high. The secret is an electromagnetic element that only heats the pan and its contents; the cooktop surface stays cool. The element even shuts itself off when the pan is removed! Ricky Moore (large photo, right), who is the head of the meat station, enjoys the safety—and cool temperature—of the new equipment.

You can eat pizza and watch a full-screen movie at the same time at the Bethesda Theatre Café in Maryland. To speed up their service, the waitstaff uses computerized wands (small photo, left center) to send the customers' orders directly to the kitchen.

Restaurant kitchens can be noisy! Chef Robert Kinkead (small photo, near left) had an idea. At Kinkead's, his Washington, D.C., restaurant, staff members communicate with the kinds of headphones that drive-through restaurants use.

In the Kitchen at
Tavern on the Green

Tavern on the Green, a New York City landmark in Central Park, does everything in a big way. Each year, 100,000 fresh flowers are delivered to the restaurant. Eighty-one chandeliers illuminate 850 seats in 6 different dining rooms. Hundreds of thousands of tiny white lights outline the trees and shrubbery around the entrance. Eleven telephone operators take reservations from 500,000 diners annually, who are served by 128 waiters.

The *Zagat Survey* of New York City restaurants has described it as a "wonderful, glitzy, glittery extravaganza."

It wasn't always that way. Built in 1870, the Victorian structure originally housed 200 sheep that were let out daily to graze in Central Park. The building became a restaurant in 1934. Now open 365 days a year for lunch and dinner, the Tavern is an incredibly busy place—as dishwasher Elpirio Santosalla (small photo, far left) could tell you. His job is to keep cutlery and plates clean. On a typical night, the Tavern serves more than 1,000 people. Can you imagine how many utensils Santosalla cleans each evening?

Tavern on the Green's kitchen operates on the brigade system—a precise organization style that is modeled on a military operation. Each restaurant worker, from the garde-manger to the pastry chef, has an assigned job. For example, William Alicea cooks mass quantities of vegetables in steaming vats (bottom right). He's a *saucier*, whose job in the brigade is to create meat, fish, and vegetable stocks or broths and then turn them into soups or sauces.

The Tavern's former executive chef, Patrick Clark (now deceased), shown at right sampling a sauce with sous-chef Stephen Moise, was one of the most famous African American chefs in the country. Tavern on the Green and its new executive chef, Rudy Sodamin, continue the traditions that make the enterprise one of the most popular restaurants in the United States. Maybe someday you'll get to eat—or even to cook—there.

Busy night. *Prep cook Christino De-Jesus (left) spends his shift in the brigade system performing his specialty. He prepares and cuts up hundreds and hundreds of vegetables—like these thinly sliced eggplants, which will be grilled in olive oil.*

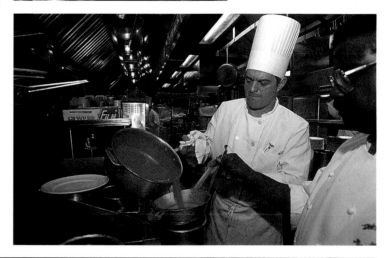

Line 'em up. *Hot-line cook Chris Brock (above) prepares a series of seven identical dishes of grilled salmon for eager diners.*

Did You Know . . .

. . . that it is important to eat lots of healthy foods, such as the vegetables, fruits, beans, and nuts shown in the photograph on the facing page? The United States Department of Agriculture recommends eating three to five servings of vegetables, two to four servings of fruit, and two to three servings of dried beans or nuts every day. This will help you maintain your ideal weight, as well as lower your risk for heart disease and some cancers.

. . . that, according to the United States Food and Drug Administration, the most desired vegetables are, in order of popularity: potatoes, iceberg lettuce, tomatoes, onions, carrots, celery, corn, broccoli, cabbage, and cucumbers?

. . . that Japanese teenagers love to munch on Calmond, a mixture of slivered almonds and dried sardines? This snack is a good source of protein and calcium.

. . . that soul food, traditional Black American cooking, originated in the cuisines of Africa and the Caribbean?

. . . that popcorn originated in Central America and was eaten by Native Americans? Popcorn six thousand years old has been found in caves in Mexico. Today the average American consumer eats forty-seven quarts of popcorn per year.

. . . that saffron is the stigma of the autumn crocus flower? Some fourteen thousand handpicked stigmas make up one ounce of saffron. This most expensive spice can cost as much as $365 per pound.

. . . that although a hamburger is the favorite main course in the United States, Americans eat more than 100 acres of pizza each day?

. . . that 1.5 billion people in the world eat with knife, fork, and spoon, 1.2 billion with chopsticks, and all other people with their hands?

. . . that cooked broccoli, seasoned with onion, cumin, and coriander, was a favorite dish at ancient Roman banquets? Try it. You might like it!

. . . that on an average day 2,160,000 Hershey's Kisses are made?

. . . that the University of Wisconsin publishes a quarterly newsletter about edible bugs called *The Food Insects Newsletter*?

HORS D'OEUVRES

Hors d'oeuvres are bite-sized portions of savory foods, served before a meal. Platters of hot and cold hors d'oeuvres are often passed at parties. The French word *hors* means "outside," and *oeuvre* means "main work." So the name tells you that this food is meant to be served separately from the main course of a formal meal.

SAUTÉ

Sautéing is a method of cooking quickly in a shallow pan over high heat, using a small amount of butter or oil. Usually the pan is heated before the butter or oil is added. Then the food goes in. The French verb *sauter* means "to jump." When an accomplished chef sautés something, instead of stirring it with a spoon, he or she will shake the hot pan, making the contents jump.

PETITS FOURS

Petits fours are bite-sized treats that are shaped in squares, diamonds, or circles. These individual cakes are glazed with several layers of icing and then decorated with chocolate or candy flowers. The French name means "little ovens." These goodies got their name because the square version of the small cakes is shaped like an old-fashioned oven.

CONVECTION OVEN

Many chefs prefer to use convection ovens rather than conventional ovens like the one you probably have in your kitchen at home. Convection ovens have fans that constantly circulate hot air around the food, cooking it evenly and more quickly than conventional ovens. Convection ovens are especially good for baking cakes and breads.

JULIENNE

Julienne foods have been sliced into very thin strips about one-eighth inch wide by one to two inches long. Salad and soup recipes often call for julienne carrots, peppers, potatoes, or other vegetables. Julienne meat is a popular ingredient in stir-fry because it cooks quickly. *Julienne* may also be used as a verb. If a recipe asks you to julienne something, simply cut it into thin strips.

TOQUE

The traditional tall white hats worn by chefs, called toques, became popular in the 1820s. There are various stories about how these hats originated. Some people say that they are a white version of the black hats that priests wore long ago. Others think that they resemble crowns and were a sign of being honored by a king. Whatever their origin, toques now stand for a special professional—the chef.

Competitions

Blue ribbons. *Sisters Amanda and Elizabeth LaBreque are ribbon winners in just about every state fair they enter. In 1997, Amanda, then twelve, won "best of show" for her yummy yellow cake.*

Sweet victory. *Jonathan Knapp, nineteen, of Fort Hill, South Carolina, was the 1997 grand-prize winner in Johnson & Wales University's "healthful dessert" category for his mango tart and chocolate banana scones.*

Chefs of all ages enjoy entering cooking competitions. It is a great way to showcase your skills, meet other chefs, find out how your culinary creations compare to other chefs' concoctions—and sometimes win valuable prizes.

A New York City organization called the Careers through Culinary Arts Program (C-CAP) runs competitions nationwide for inner-city high school students (below left). Winners earn scholarships to cooking schools, including the Culinary Institute of America and the Swiss Hospitality Institute. The world's largest culinary school—Johnson & Wales University in Providence, Rhode Island—conducts an annual recipe contest for high school students. Twenty finalists from around the country are flown each year to a daylong cook-off. Can you guess what first-place winner Jonathan Knapp's prize was? A four-year scholarship to Johnson & Wales.

Amanda and Elizabeth LaBreque (above left)

Future chefs. *Some ten thousand students are enrolled in the C-CAP program. It has already awarded more than $3 million in scholarships to talented chefs-to-be.*

Hot lunch. *Middle school students assist professional chefs at the American Culinary Federation's annual School Lunch Challenge in Atlanta, Georgia, to improve school lunch menus.*

have been entering their baked goods in regional and state fairs for several years—and winning prizes. Amanda won her first blue ribbon for oatmeal cookies when she was only six. In 1997 she won the grand-champion and best-of-show ribbons at the Loudoun County Fair in Virginia. She and her sister are still collecting honors.

Sometimes chefs compete for the honor of winning a prestigious award. In the photo above, executive chef Kevin E. Donovan puts the finishing touches on an appetizer at a regional tryout for the American Culinary Federation's "Team 2000." Regional winners move one step closer to being on a team of chefs that will represent the United States in international culinary competitions into the twenty-first century.

Critical eye. The judge assessing Kevin Donovan's hors d'oeuvre (left) gave him good marks. Kevin, who is a chef at a country club when he isn't winning contests, won a medal and advanced to the national competition.

Dishes from around the World

One of the benefits of being a chef is learning about cuisines from other countries. Many chefs say that traveling abroad and sampling unfamiliar foods is an important part of their continuing education. By exploring world cuisine, chefs discover new ways to use spices and other ingredients, and by trying new and exotic flavors, they get to stimulate their tastebuds.

Are you an aspiring chef? Be adventurous! Visit restaurants to taste authentic ethnic dishes. Then check out cookbooks of world cuisines and try the recipes yourself.

TACOS AND TAMALES A Mexican specialty, the thin cornmeal tortillas often filled with meat, beans, cheese, and chilies were first developed by the Olmecs in 1500 B.C.

SUSHI The Japanese love the delicate taste of raw fish—especially accompanied by a touch of powerful wasabi (similar to horseradish), a dash of soy sauce, and a sliver of pickled gingerroot.

KUNG PAO SHRIMP. This spicy Chinese dish combines peanuts, vegetables, shrimp, and dried chilies, and is served with rice.

WAT This Ethiopian stew, which consists of an array of spicy meat and vegetables, is served with fresh fruit and flat doughy bread called *injera*.

MOUSSAKA Layers of meat, eggplant, and potatoes covered with a light cream sauce called béchamel make up this hearty Greek dish.

SAUERBRATEN This German specialty of beef marinated and then cooked in a red wine sauce is often served with tangy sauerkraut and mild dumplings.

PASTA *PRIMAVERA* The Italians make hundreds of different pasta dishes. This one features spring vegetables.

PAELLA A Spanish dish cooked in a cast-iron skillet, paella includes rice, seafood, and saffron, a delicate spice.

APPLE PIE In the United States, this pie is so popular that people call familiar things "as American as apple pie."

ESCARGOTS The French love this classic dish of cooked snails served in the shell and drenched in garlic butter.

GOULASH A Hungarian meat stew, goulash is flavored with lots of paprika and served with vegetables and noodles.

MI A flavorful combination of broth, noodles, vegetables, and seafood, *mi* is a popular meal in Vietnam.

FEIJOADA This well-known Brazilian dish—a mixture of black beans, meats, collard greens, rice, and fruit—actually originated in Africa.

COUSCOUS In Morocco, people eat couscous—ground semolina, flour, and water—served with meat, vegetables, and chickpeas.

TANDOORI CHICKEN This spicy Indian dish, served with rice and condiments, is cooked in a very hot oven called a tandoor.

Related Careers

There are lots of ways to work with food—your career may not take you into a busy restaurant or hotel kitchen. Food service—and food science—offer many choices. You could be a freelance baker like Andrea Webster, who works at home, in Washington, D.C. At top right, she carefully adds an icing rose to a cake. Many of her wedding cakes, like this one, are inspired by bridal gowns and real flowers. Webster believes in making special-occasion cakes from scratch, using the finest ingredients. "A cake should taste as good as—if not better than—it looks," she says.

Could you eat pizza three times a day? Then you'll probably envy Al Rose (right, second from top). As a menu development manager for Domino's Pizza in Chicago, Illinois, he munches about one thousand slices a year, testing combinations of sauce, dough, and toppings to help Domino's bring new products to the market.

Quality is important to Adrian Hughes, executive assistant manager in charge of the food and beverage division at the Hyatt Regency Hotel in Washington, D.C. He is responsible for ensuring that food delivered to the hotel is of the highest quality and freshness. At right, second from bottom, he inspects a delivery of asparagus.

Some chefs love to teach. Chef-instructor Joel Olson (bottom right) enjoys his position as director of children's programs at L'Académie de Cuisine in Bethesda, Maryland.

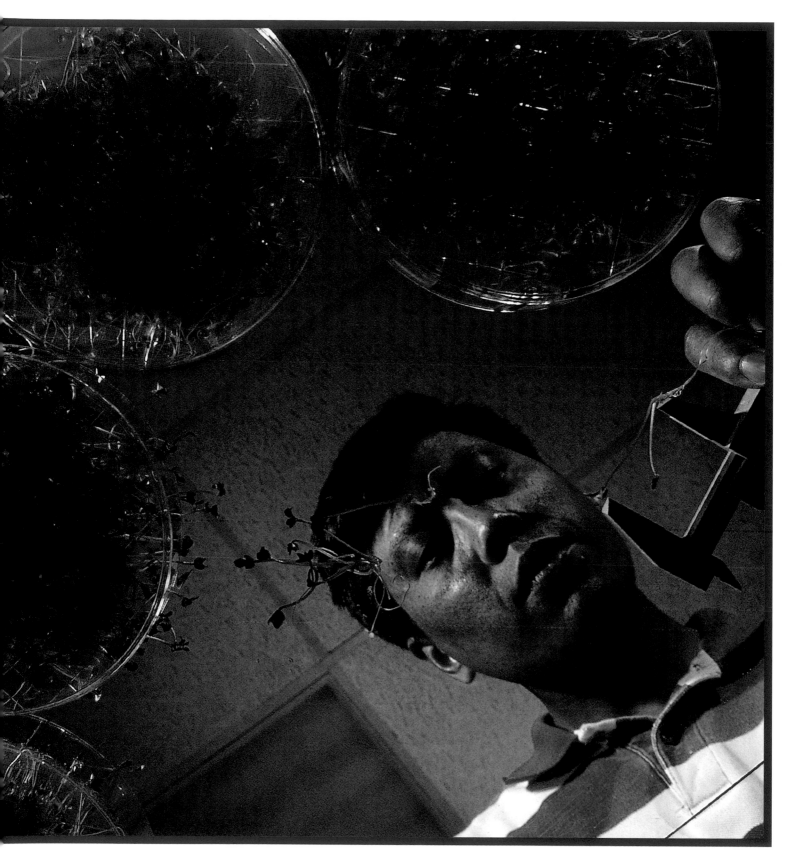

Basic food chemistry. Researcher Yuesheng Zhang (above) at Johns Hopkins University in Baltimore, Maryland, and colleagues discovered that three-day-old broccoli sprouts contain a powerful cancer-fighting compound.

The sprouts became available to consumers in 1997. At the lab, researchers often eat broccoli sprouts for a healthful midmorning snack as they work on discovering other disease-fighting foods.

Entrepreneurs

Some success stories don't begin with graduation from an elite culinary school or an apprenticeship at a fancy French restaurant. Some stories are dreams that come true because of creative thinking, a little luck, and a lot of hard work. In these pages, you'll meet people who have started their own food businesses—and are making them work. They're entrepreneurs, people who organize, operate, and assume the financial risk for their own businesses.

At left, Linda Fisher, the "muffin lady," mixes batter in the kitchen at the volunteer fire department in Westminster, Maryland. She used to run her small baking business out of her home, trying hard to earn enough money to avoid going on welfare. She would bake early in the morning then pack up her muffins in a little red wagon that she used to deliver her treats to customers. When the state of Maryland told her she would have to get permits and work in an inspected kitchen, Fisher worried that she'd have to shut down. But townspeople rallied to help her do the paperwork for the permits. And the firehouse donated its kitchen, which meets state sanitation standards. Soon the muffin lady's red wagon was rolling through the streets of Westminster again. Now she has even written a cookbook!

Miguel Jara, shown preparing a soft taco in the small picture at right center, launched a small business in San Francisco's Mission district

Spice lady. *Ann Wilder, owner of Vanns Spices Ltd., a wholesale spice company in Baltimore, Maryland, started her business from home to sell pungent tandoori seasoning. Today Vanns sells many spices from its large warehouse.*

Sushi man. *Until recently, Chef Kazuhiro Okaochi (left) was head sushi chef and co-owner of Sushi-Ko in Washington, D.C., one of the first restaurants in the nation's capital to specialize in the raw fish delicacies.*

that celebrates a traditional Mexican food: tacos to go. Small, portable, and quick to make, tacos are ideal take-out food. Business is booming at La Taqueria!

Chris and Mary Gluck of San Diego, California, love pasta so much that they've built their professional lives around it as publishers of *Pasta Press: The Magazine for Connoisseurs of Fine Pasta.* Daughter Erica, eleven (center photo at right), an aspiring chef, also got into the act. As the magazine's children's editor, she writes a kids' column that features fun recipes tested by kids. They come with simple explanations and kitchen pointers for young cooks. The recipes are healthy, too—every one gets less than 20 percent of its calories from fat. Erica runs her own business, selling fresh, flavored pastas at farmers' markets. She also enjoys cooking with her dad. What are they making? You guessed it: pasta!

Robert Egger (bottom right, second from right), shown with volunteer cooks, used his entrepreneurial skills to do something special. He founded D.C. Central Kitchen, a nonprofit organization that prepares 2,500 free meals a day, 365 days a year, to feed hungry people. D.C. Central Kitchen provides meals for homeless individuals, after-school programs, youth centers, and senior citizen groups. Where does the food come from? That was one of Egger's great ideas: He gets surplus food from caterers, restaurants, hotels, and other food service businesses. More than 25 tons of food is donated each month from 1,500 establishments.

Brainstorms. *Eugene Kinlow (facing page, top) knew that people loved fried chicken, and thought, Why not fried turkey? So he started Mr. DeWitt's Fried Turkeys in Washington, D.C. The deep-fried whole birds make unusual holiday meals. Susan Schindler of BrainWash, a café-Laundromat in San Francisco (above), had a brain wave. She knew that people get hungry while they wait for laundry to dry. So why not feed them? She teamed up with chef Gloria Lucero-Buschman to offer customers baked goods, sandwiches, and more. At right, stylist Norman streaks Lynn Cooley's hair as she eats at H Design, a bakery-deli-beauty salon, in Minneapolis, Minnesota.*

World Cuisine

If you could plan a trip abroad, where would you go? What would you see? What would you eat and drink? People who go to faraway places find that one of the great adventures of travel is discovering the restaurants, markets, and specialty food shops in other countries. Experience overseas expands chefs' minds and refreshes their taste buds. For these reasons, many American chefs choose to spend at least some time training in restaurants abroad.

On these pages, take a brief tour of some culinary specialties from around the world. In the background is the beautiful Douro River region of Portugal, where sweet port wine is made in the same way it has been for centuries. Above left, Spanish pastry chef Jose Balcells Pallares can't resist licking the bowl as he poses with an 8-foot, 229-pound chocolate Statue of Liberty, which he sculpted. Above right, chefs prepare a more traditional Spanish meal, paella, in a fish restaurant on the Costa Brava. Spanish workers in Catalonia (opposite page, top left) process grapes at Cordonia after the harvest. The fruit will eventually be transformed into sparkling wine. At top far right, a vendor displays a variety of vegetables at an open-air market in Indonesia. Picture the julienne salad an imaginative chef could create with them!

International specialties. *An Italian confectioner makes confetti—sugar-coated almonds traditionally served at weddings (near right). In the Jamaica Market in Mexico City, a vendor displays piles of fresh corn (right center)— a staple in Central America since the time of the Aztecs. At far right, a French shopkeeper holds a wheel of delectable Brie at a* fromagerie, *a store that sells only cheese.*

Some Famous Chefs

Individual chefs can become well known for the cooking styles they develop. On these pages, meet some influential chefs whose creativity and talents have changed the way we eat.

◀ PATRICK CLARK

Born in Brooklyn, New York, Clark was one of the best-known and most influential American chefs. When he was young, he wanted to be a chef like his father, who cooked at the Four Seasons Hotel. Clark trained at New York City Technical College and then apprenticed at famous restaurants in England and France. At high-profile U.S. restaurants, such as Tavern on the Green in New York City, he became known for fusing French and American cuisine. The world lost a creative culinary leader when Patrick Clark died in 1998.

◀ EMERIL LAGASSE

You can catch this chef's show, *Emeril Live*, on the cable TV Food Network. In front of a live audience, Lagasse demonstrates how to cook spicy Louisiana recipes with his own special touch of down-home humor. He also owns Emeril's and Nola, in New Orleans, and Emeril's New Orleans Fish House, in Las Vegas.

◀ ZARELA MARTINEZ

The chef-owner of the popular restaurant Zarela's in New York City, Martinez is one of the leading Mexican cooks in the United States. She writes cookbooks, caters, and gives Mexican cooking lessons. She is also a founder of Mexico Diverso, an organization dedicated to protecting Mexican cultural and biological diversity.

JACQUES TORRES ▶

When he was named the Meilleur Ouvrier de France Pâtissier (best pastry chef) in his native France at age twenty-six, Torres became one of the youngest chefs ever to receive this honor. Now pastry chef at Le Cirque, in New York City, he also teaches at the French Culinary Institute.

SUSANNA FOO ▶

Born in China and raised in Taiwan, Foo came to the United States to become a librarian. Instead, she decided to become a chef. With her husband, she opened Susanna Foo Chinese Cuisine in Philadelphia, where she combines Chinese and non-Chinese traditions in unique recipes.

LARRY FORGIONE ▲
Chef-owner of An American Place, in New York City, and the Beekman Tavern, in Rhinebeck, New York, Forgione is a graduate of the Culinary Institute of America. An expert on American cooking, he's the author of the influential *America Itself: An American Harvest Cookbook*.

EDNA LEWIS ▼
A native of Virginia, Edna Lewis is considered the world's foremost authority on American southern cooking. Her best-selling cookbooks (she started writing her fourth one in her eighties!) and her work as chef at Gage & Tollner in Brooklyn, New York, made southern cooking popular all over the country.

PAUL BOCUSE ▲
In the 1960s, Bocuse invented nouvelle cuisine, a style of French cooking that uses less butter and cream than traditional French cooking and emphasizes fresh, healthful ingredients. Nouvelle cuisine has changed the way people eat in Europe and the United States.

MADELEINE KAMMAN ▲
Born in Paris and taught to cook by her family, Kamman moved to the United States in 1960 and quickly popularized her style of French home cooking through her restaurants, cookbooks, and PBS television show, *Madeleine Cooks*. She is now director of the School for American Chefs in California's Napa Valley.

MARK MILLER ▼
A former student of anthropology, Miller became known for popularizing southwestern cuisine—through his cookbooks, chile posters, and his many Coyote Cafés in New Mexico, Texas, and Nevada. He is also known for his Asian restaurants Raku of Washington, D.C., and Bethesda, Maryland, as well as Lōongbar of San Francisco, California.

NOBUYUKI MATSUHISA ▲
A native of Japan, Matsuhisa now commutes around the world to run restaurants he owns in Los Angeles, New York City, and London. He will soon open new restaurants in Tokyo and in Aspen, Colorado, where he will continue to serve modern adaptations of classical Japanese dishes—including sushi.

You Can Be a Chef!

Has this book inspired you to get into the kitchen and try out some recipes? It's never too early to start cooking. Justin Miller, eight, of Baden, Pennsylvania, has been working with food since he was a toddler. He published his first cookbook, *Cooking with Justin,* in 1997. When he cooks, Justin does his own cleanup. He has cooked on the *Late Show with David Letterman,* has produced a pilot television show that features cooking and ecology, and has met many famous chefs. But right now Justin isn't limiting himself to one career choice. "I want to be a chef and a pilot," he says.

Try this treat from Justin's cookbook:

MINI CHEESECAKES

3 8-ounce tubs whipped
   cream cheese
3 eggs
½ cup sugar
1 teaspoon vanilla extract

1 heaping tablespoon flour
1 box Vanilla Wafers
1 12-oz. can cherry or blueberry
   pie filling
12 mini cupcake cups

Preheat oven to 350 degrees. Mix the cream cheese, eggs, sugar, vanilla, and flour in a blender. Blend until smooth. Arrange the cupcake cups in a muffin tin or baking dish. Place one Vanilla Wafer flat side down into each cup. With a serving spoon, scoop a small amount of the mixture from the blender and place on top of one wafer; fill the cup about halfway. (Leave room for the cheesecake to rise.) Repeat until all of the batter is gone. Place cheesecakes in the oven and bake for 20 minutes. Cool completely and top with the pie filling.

"This is my favorite recipe," says Justin. "I like to make it for my friends at school."

This book has introduced you to lots of chefs and showed you examples of places where cooks-in-training learn their trade. To find out more about the world of cooking and culinary careers, turn the page.

Other Sources of Information

CULINARY ORGANIZATIONS:

American Culinary Federation
P.O. Box 3466
St. Augustine, FL 32085

This is the major professional organization for chefs in the United States. It accredits postsecondary education programs for chefs, gives awards, and maintains an honor society. Its magazine, the National Culinary Review, *is read by chefs around the world.*

American Institute of Baking (AIB)
1213 Bakers Way
Manhattan, KS 66502

This nonprofit educational organization promotes education in nutrition and in the science and art of baking and bakery management.

Careers through Culinary Arts Program, Inc. (C-CAP)
155 West 68th Street
New York, NY 10023

This group's membership consists of 10,000 students in 190 schools in Arizona, California, Illinois, New York, Pennsylvania, Virginia, and Washington, D.C. C-CAP is a nonprofit corporation that promotes and provides career opportunities in the food service industry for inner-city youth through culinary arts education and apprenticeship programs.

International Association of Culinary Professionals
304 West Liberty Street, Suite 201
Louisville, KY 40202

With nearly 4,000 members worldwide, IACP represents virtually every profession in the culinary field. A "who's who" of the food professions, the IACP members list includes cooking teachers, food writers, chefs, caterers, restaurateurs, TV cooking personalities, editors and publishers, and leaders of major food corporations.

International Association of Women Chefs and Restaurateurs
110 Sutter Street, Suite 210
San Francisco, CA 94104

This group promotes the education and advancement of women in the restaurant industry.

James Beard Foundation
167 West 12th Street
New York, NY 10011

This foundation—formed to honor chef James Beard, the "Father of American Cooking"—promotes the appreciation of American cuisine.

National Restaurant Association
1200 17th Street NW
Washington, DC 20036

This association provides its members—people who work in restaurants—with continuing education and services, including an annual conference.

Oldways Preservation & Exchange Trust
25 First Street
Cambridge, MA 02141

This group preserves the healthy, environmentally appropriate food traditions of many cultures.

A SELECTION OF PROFESSIONAL COOKING SCHOOLS:

Baltimore International College
17 Commerce Street
Baltimore, MD 21202

California Culinary Academy
625 Polk Street
San Francisco, CA 94102

The Cooking and Hospitality Institute of Chicago
361 West Chestnut
Chicago, IL 60610

The Culinary Institute of America
433 Albany Post Road
Hyde Park, NY 12538

The Florida Culinary Institute
1126 53rd Court
West Palm Beach, FL 33407

The French Culinary Institute
462 Broadway
New York, NY 10013

International Culinary Academy
107 Sixth Street
Pittsburgh, PA 15222

Johnson & Wales University
8 Abbott Park Place
Providence, RI 02903

L'Académie de Cuisine
5021 Wilson Lane
Bethesda, MD 20814

Metropolitan College at Boston University
808 Commonwealth Avenue
Boston, MA 02215

The Natural Gourmet Cookery School
48 West 21st Street, 2nd Floor
New York, NY 10010

New England Culinary Institute
250 Main Street, Dept. S
Montpelier, VT 05602

New York Food and Hotel Management School
154 West 14th Street, 11th Floor
New York, NY 10011

The Restaurant School
4207 Walnut Street
Philadelphia, PA 19104

Scottsdale Culinary Institute
8100 Camelback Road, Suite 1001
Scottsdale, AZ 85251

Western Culinary Institute
1316 Southwest 13th Avenue
Portland, OR 97201

Many community colleges award degrees in the culinary arts. Check under EDUCATION *in your local* Yellow Pages *to locate the community colleges in your area. Call them to find out about their programs.*

MAGAZINES AND OTHER RESOURCES:

Radcliffe Culinary Friends Schlesinger Library at Radcliffe College
10 Garden Street
Cambridge, MA 02138

This group collects, catalogs, and preserves books and magazines related to food. The collection has about ten thousand works in the field of cookery, dating from the sixteenth century to the present.

Bon Appétit
6300 Wilshire Boulevard
Los Angeles, CA 90048

Chef
20 North Wacker, Suite 1865
Chicago, IL 60606

Cook's Illustrated
17 Station Street, Box 1200
Brookline, MA 02147

Gourmet
560 Lexington Avenue
New York, NY 10022

Saveur
100 Avenue of the Americas
New York, NY 10013

Becoming a Chef
by Andrew Dornenburg and Karen Page

A comprehensive book about what it is really like to become a chef. Includes recipes and reflections from America's leading chefs.

PHOTO CREDITS